Surviving Against All Odds

Surviving Against All Odds

One Woman's Testimony of Survival

by
Nicole Quiroz

XULON PRESS

Xulon Press
2301 Lucien Way #415
Maitland, FL 32751
407.339.4217
www.xulonpress.com

© 2020 by Nicole Quiroz

Printed in the United States of America.

ISBN-13: 978-1-6312-9742-7
Ebook: 978-1-6312-9743-4

Warning!

The contents in this book may be disturbing to some readers. The author depicts real life situations that may be upsetting to the reader.

This book is dedicated to:

God for His unending love and faithfulness
My husband for his unwavering commitment
My children for walking this journey with me
My family of friends for their loving support
Those who still have to walk this difficult road

Table of Contents

Chapter One

◦◦◦

Most of my childhood was spent holding my breath, waiting for the next emotional bomb to hit. Bad memories, by far, outnumbered the good ones. By the age of twelve, I found myself the blunt of many children's jokes. I was socially awkward, and I found it difficult to fit in and hard to relate to the other kids, even though all I ever wanted was to fit in with the popular ones. I would daydream that many kids in school liked me. As I passed kids in the hallway, they would know me by name and say hi to me. Walking down the hallway, I would be jerked back into reality as another student bumped into me and called me a name. I didn't have many friends, and I was a bit of an outcast. On many occasions, I would get a pass from the teacher to go to the bathroom and just cry in the stall. The jokes and taunting made me feel horrible. What the kids in school didn't understand about me was that I was holding on to a deep secret. I finally confided in one girl in school and told her about what was happening to me at home. She told her mom, who was the secretary of our school, but not before telling everyone in our class. In a moment of desperation, I had shared with this girl that my stepfather was abusing me. From that moment on, things became worse for me.

Child protection was called by the secretary of the school. They came to my home for a visit. My stepfather was one really good and talented smooth talker; he was able to talk his way right out of trouble. It also helped that I had no visible bruises. This was one of many visits that child protection would make to my home. I remember imagining that someone would come and rescue me and take me away from all the pain, hurt, and anguish that I was feeling. However, no one ever came, and I began to give up on that fairy tale ending.

My stepfather's name was Tom, but I was to call him Dad. Growing up, this was a bit confusing for me because I had a real dad who was otherwise detained in prison. He had committed crimes that landed him a ten-year stretch. Periodically, I would see my real father when my grandmother would take me to visit him at the prison. It was a long drive, and I only saw him maybe once every few months. I would often go to my grandmother's on the weekends, per my mother and father's visitation agreement. The only father that I really knew was Tom.

As a child, if someone had asked me to explain Tom to them, I would only have one word: monster! To me, he was a monster, and I feared him like I would a real-life monster. But in reality, although he was very cruel, he was still just a man. He was overweight and had a huge beer gut that made him look like he was nine-months pregnant. He was a drunk and drank on a regular basis. I'm not sure if he would be categorized as a nice drunk or a mean drunk because when he drank, you never knew what you were going to get. He smoked cigarettes, which gave him a raspy voice. He was always coughing, and when he coughed, his whole face would turn beet red. On occasion, I witnessed him snorting coke with his friends. We would often go with Tom and my mother camping at all-night parties. I remember on one specific occasion, while camping, Tom touching me inappropriately. The music was loud, and I could not sleep. When my mom and Tom came to sleep in the tent, I was between them. Tom began to touch me in my private areas while I was pretending to sleep. I remember just lying there, not knowing what to do. I just lay still until it was over.

Living with Tom was like waiting for a big storm to hit. I would see the signs; his temperament would change. He would go from content to angry very fast, like raindrops quickly turning to showers. His words would strike like lightning, and before I knew it, thunder would hit and he would explode. I never knew when the storm would come or how long it would last. I would run to my room, hoping to find some shelter from the storm, but it always found me. There was no avoiding it. Yet after the storm, everything would go quiet, and calm would once again be restored. The only reminisce of the storm was the teardrops that streamed down my face.

My mom worked and went to school, so Tom was my main caretaker. He was a neat freak, and everything had to be perfect. My room was always to be clean and could never get dirty. Tom believed that children were to be seen and not heard, so I was to be as quiet as possible when playing in my room. I spent most of my time playing in my room and rarely went downstairs unless I had to. There was one girl from school that I was allowed to visit; she lived around the corner. I would go to her house for maybe an hour or so, and it would be like an escape for the day. Her parents were nice, and she was ok. She didn't really like me, and I am not sure that I really liked her. Still, going to her house meant getting away from Tom, so I was all for it.

At times, Tom could be extremely cruel. He would tell me on a daily basis that I was fat, ugly, and that no one would ever love me. He said this so many times that I began to believe him. One of his other favorite things was to kick my rear end all the way up the stairs as I struggled to get away. When it was time to eat, he would put a large amount of food on my plate and tell me to eat all of it or else. If I didn't eat fast enough, he would jab his pointer finger between my shoulder blades.

One time, when I watched his son's kids while he went out drinking, an awful incident happened. His son came back really late the next morning, so I didn't get home until after that. Later that day, Tom's son came over and told Tom that I was lying, that he had not been out that late. Tom was furious with me. I tried to tell him that his son was lying, but he wouldn't believe me. He chased me up the stairs, kicking me in my rear the whole way. I got a little ahead of him and ran to my room and slammed the door. He came right behind me and slammed his hand against the door. In his anger, he didn't realize that there was a nail right there in the door. That made him even angrier as he came into my room, bleeding from his hand. His face was red like fire, and he was screaming at me. He grabbed a hold of me and started throwing me around the room. He tore my shirt off of me and made me clean his blood off of the floor with my shirt. As I struggled to get away, he choked me. Finally, he must have realized what he was doing and let his hands off of my throat. That was one of the times I thought he was going to beat me to death.

More than anything he ever did to me, Tom's words hurt me the most. He used to tell me that I got my freckles from standing behind the fence while the cows were having a shit fight. As a result, I hated my freckles so much that I tried to shave them off my face. I used to spend a lot of time in the bathroom, trying to make potions that would take my freckles away. I would mix shampoos and soaps and believe that when I woke in the morning, my freckles would be gone. I would always be disappointed when I woke up and saw that they were still there. I had a doll that had a fabric face with freckles like me, and I shaved off her freckles. I don't think that I could have hated myself any more than I did.

Even though Tom caused me such anguish, I loved him as my dad. He had moments when he would be so nice to me and let me stay up and watch TV, usually a very inappropriate movie. We watched one movie that was so violent that I can still remember it today. Often after a beating, he would seem to try to make up for what he had done with TV. Another time, he surprised me in the car by putting a stuffed animal in a coffee mug and handed it to me. I was so excited that he had surprised me with the toy and felt really special at that moment. My mom was in the car with us, so I don't know if he was doing it to show my mom what a great guy he was or if he genuinely wanted to do something special for me. He also would fix my hair before school. He would braid it and put it up nice. When he would do my hair, it was one of the only times I didn't find myself holding my breath, waiting for him to go off.

One of the very worst episodes with Tom was when I was doing the dishes and left a spot on a dish. The dishes were my job, and I was to wash them completely, leaving nothing on them. This time in particular, something in him must have snapped. He grabbed a butcher knife and started screaming at me and waving the knife. I was so scared that I ran outside. He came to the screen door and told me to get my ass back in the house now! I was so scared that I did what he told me and came back into the house. He pulled me into the laundry room and began taunting me with the knife. The more scared I became, the angrier he got. I was sure he was going to kill me. He then lured me into the basement, where he raped me on the basement floor.

Shortly after this episode, it happened again. I had been washing the dishes when Tom grabbed the knife and chased me with it. Once again, I ran outside, and he yelled and threatened me to come back inside. I was so scared of what he was going to do to me that I ran. I ran and I ran all the way to my mom's friend's house. The whole time, I was wondering what Tom was going to do to me for running away. I have never again felt the fear that I felt that day. My mom's friend called my mom, who came from work to get me. She never made me go back there again. She left Tom that day, and I would not see him again for many years.

LEFT

It's a dark and deserted place where you left my heart,
Alone and torn apart.
You took what you wanted from me,
Then you left to flee
Away from any questions of why,
Or stay present to see what went awry.
You didn't see the aftermath
Of your choice and path.
Now I'm left living with the residue of your sins.
In this situation, who really wins?
You can't bring yourself to face the truth,

While I'm left with a pain nothing on this earth can sooth.

A short time after leaving Tom, my mom introduced me to her new boyfriend. He seemed really nice, and my mom was really happy. It wasn't long before my mom became worried that I was not doing well, emotionally. She had decided that the only option was to send me away to get help. The children's home that they had planned on sending me to did not have an opening, and I was sent a few different places before I was sent to the children's home. I was first sent to two different detention centers, then a psychiatric hospital and a foster home. Finally, I was placed in the children's home. In the detention centers, most of the children were there for behavior problems, but I was not there for that reason. My mom and her boyfriend only put me in the detention centers because there was nowhere else to place me at the time. The first detention center I was in was not far from my home. Since the kids in the detention center weren't in public school. They homeschooled us. I made friends that I would soon have to leave. The staff was really nice and treated me well, and every once in a while, my mom and her boyfriend would come to visit me.

The second detention center was further from my home, so I did not get any visitors. I don't recall, but I think there may have been a rule against visitors coming. I do remember that while I was there, no other kids had any visitors. It wasn't bad there either. The staff was nice, and I got along with the other kids well. We weren't supposed to be able to call anyone from home, but on my birthday, I was surprised when I was called into the office and handed the phone. My mom was on the other end. She and my brother wished me a happy birthday. I was handed some cards that were sent from home. It was nice to get them, and I felt cared about on my birthday. I was surprised again when the staff at the detention center handed me a card that all the kids had made and signed for me. That night, the staff on duty let me stay up late and watch a movie. That was a good memory of my birthday. The people from the detention center made my birthday matter, which helped lessen my sadness about being away from home.

The man at the detention center who let me stay up late was a young black man who would be my first contact with a good man. After allowing me to stay up and watch the movie, he tucked me into bed and said goodnight and that he hoped my birthday was special. I kissed this young man on the mouth, thinking that I needed to repay him because he had been nice to me. He said to me that I was just a child and that I didn't need to repay him for what he had done for me. With tears in his eyes, he told me that I deserved to feel special without feeling like I had to repay his kindness. I was embarrassed by my actions, but this man helped me to feel better about it and comforted me when I started crying after realizing I had done something wrong. He was a good man, and that night, I learned that there were good men in the world.

From the detention center, I was sent to a psychiatric hospital. It was not as nice there, but the staff didn't treat me badly. There were a lot of other kids there who were fighting depression and other issues. We were home-schooled there as well, and they had activities for us to do. I remember we would earn "mall bucks" that we could spend at the local mall. It wasn't so bad, but I missed home. After my stay at the psychiatric hospital, I went to a foster home. The foster home was not so good. The foster parents gave me and another girl who was staying there lists of chores to do. They didn't talk to us at all, and we mainly stayed in our room and kept each other company. One day, I asked the mother if she didn't like me and why they treated us the way they did. The next day, I was sent to Bradford Children's Home, where I would stay for one year. I had no contact with family for the first three months so that I could get used to being there. At the children's home, I made friends with the other children who were there, and the staff treated me well. They took us shopping for new clothes and made a big deal out of Christmas. We played sports and did a lot of activities.

DEAR LORD

Please take the terror and pain from me;
The memories are so jarring and won't let me be.
The truth wants to come out from deep within,
Exposing my reality and their sin.
I want it not to be real
Because of all inside that it will reveal
About my life and worth.

Was I not wanted from birth?
How can it be
That no one could see
The terror I was living for so long?
Until one day I was finally gone,
Away from the hurt and pain
To another place where love didn't reign.

After a year in the children's home at the age of 13, I was placed in their girls' group home, which was so much fun. Although we were homeschooled, we had a prom. It was the only prom I ever experienced. I remember dressing up in our fancy dresses and dancing with our dates. The dates were of course boys who were in the group homes. The staff did their best to make it a special night for us, and it really was special. I had two roommates at the girls' group home—one was a diehard Elvis Presley fan and the other loved The Doors. It was so much fun when they would bicker about who was better than whom and whose turn it was to listen to what. I would be the first girl at the girls' home to go to public school. I argued for my rights to go to public school, and I won. At the public school, it was a little hard to fit in with the other kids, but I made friends. It was also hard to keep the fact that I lived in a group home a secret from the other kids at school. If someone would invite me to come to their house for a playdate, I would have to explain that I could not because I lived in a home. That part of going to public school was difficult. I would be gone from home for a total of about three years, and I would return home sometime around the age of fifteen.

Chapter Two

⁓

When I returned home, I was still struggling to deal with the abuse. I found a group of friends who were not healthy for me, but for the first time in my life, I felt accepted. These friends introduced me to drinking alcohol and smoking cigarettes and even marijuana. It wasn't long before I started having sex. I wanted to feel loved, and having sex was one way that I could feel that—only, when it was over, I would feel even worse and struggle to look at myself in the mirror. My friends and I had our own little gang and would get together after school and drink and smoke marijuana. On the weekends, we would go to different parties, where I would end up getting plastered and sleeping with someone that I didn't really even know. I loved getting high and drinking with my friends because when I was high and drinking, everything was a party and nothing mattered…until the next day.

Soon, I became very promiscuous and would sneak out of my house at night to go to parties. After my mom and my now new step-father fell asleep. One day, after I returned home from school, my parents told me that I was grounded. My stepdad had read my diary and found out that I was doing drugs. After that, things at home just went downhill. Growing tired of my behavior, my parents kicked me out of the house, so I stayed with friends. I got a part-time job working at Burger King and started paying fifty dollars a week to stay at one friend's house. My friend was never home and did not keep food in the house, so I ended up eating a lot of relish sandwiches. Living there didn't work for me, and I soon had to leave.

I then went to the department of social services, and they helped me to get an apartment, since I was homeless and could not go back to my parents. Once I got my own place, it became a party house, and I was getting drunk almost every night. I decided to drop out of school, leaving my education and my place on the varsity volleyball team. During this time, I would go from one bad relationship to another, unable to find the love that I was seeking. I continued to drink and experiment with different drugs. I didn't like myself very much and drank away my insecurities. When I was partying with my friends, I felt good. I thought that they accepted the real me. However, I would come to realize that they were not real friends and just wanted a place to party.

RESOLUTION

I see it all, I see it so clear,
The answers I've been searching for all these years,
A buried solution that remained hidden due to fear,
Hearing that lost child as she whispers in my ear,
Spilling secrets that I held so tight,
Transforming my thoughts, filling me with anger and spite,
Looking to others to bring my happiness,
Being left with pain and emptiness,
Believing fairy tale endings
Brought relationships not fit for mending,

Left incomplete and unfulfilled,
My own destiny at my will.
Unable to fight the demons within,
My life ceases to begin
As I continue to search for the inner key
To unlock the darkness and set me free.

When I was seventeen, I decided to find Tom to confront him about the abuse from my childhood. I wanted him to tell me why he had been so cruel to me. I needed answers; I needed to know if he was sorry for what he had done to me. I also wanted to know if he had ever loved me or if he treated me the way he did because he hated me. When I asked my mom how I could track him down, she said I should go to the town where he lived, find a bar, and he would probably be there. So, I went to a bar that was on the main street in his town, but I did not find him there. I did, however, find some friends of his who took me to his house. When I walked in, Tom saw me, looked down at the floor, and went into his basement. He never came back up. He didn't look like the monster I had remembered. Instead, he was a frail old man and looked sickly, as if he was dying.

Several years later, I found out that he had died of emphysema. I never did get the answers that I was searching for.

Months after my encounter with Tom, I went to a friend's house for a party. I met a great guy at the party. After a while, we started dating. He didn't drink or do drugs, so I was able to stop partying to be with him. My parents weren't exactly happy to hear that I had decided to have a relationship with a Mexican man, but as they got to know him, they accepted him. We didn't get a very warm reception from people who saw us in public together, as many would just stare at us with disapproving looks on their faces. We knew that if we were going to be together, we would have to accept that people were not always going to be happy about it. Our relationship moved fast, and after two months of dating, we moved in together. We were very much in love and enjoyed every minute we had with each other. Nine months after meeting each other, we decided to get married. His status here in the United States was not legal, so we both feared that he may be deported. This was one of the reasons why we decided to get married so soon. We were both young and did not realize the seriousness of marriage. When we would get into an argument,

I would tell him to leave and that it was over. We went back and forth for some time; we would be together, then not together. I struggled dealing with the pressure of being married. We had different expectations of each other and of what marriage was, and I especially had a very difficult time fitting into my new role.

Several months into the marriage, I decided that I couldn't handle the pressure of being married, as I was still dealing with my past abuse. So, one morning, I took all the medicine in the medicine cabinet as an attempt to kill myself. I went out and sat on the couch, waiting for it all to end. When I started slurring my words and couldn't keep my eyes open, my husband realized that something was wrong. He went into the bathroom and saw that I had taken all of the medicine, then he called his boss to rush me to the hospital. When I woke up in the ICU, I was told that I almost didn't make it. I was kept in the psychiatric unit of the hospital for a week before I was sent back home. For three months, I was anemic and had to take iron pills. My husband did his best to help me through my depression.

After this incident, I finally decided to go back to school. I was accepted into a program that allows you to take a GED test. If you pass the first time you take it, you are eligible to get an EDP diploma from a real high school. You also have to only have a little bit of time left for graduation. I qualified for the program and began my testing. After a few months, I succeeded and was able to get my diploma. I was the first person in my family to get my high school diploma. Getting my diploma was really important to me, and I was so happy.

While I was still working on my diploma, I found out I was pregnant. My husband and I were very excited, and things were going really well for a while—until we got into a big argument and I left. I went back to live with my parents. Even though we were not together, my husband was there every step of the way. He held my hand during labor, and when the doctors decided I needed a C-section, he was right there supporting me. I had a baby boy. We were still separated, and I felt it was time for me to move out of my parent's house and into my own place. I ended up getting into a program that would furnish housing for me so that I could once again live on my own. I wanted to make a good life for my son, and decided that the best thing for me to do was to go to college and get a degree. I found a sitter for my son and started going to college. I was doing really well. During this time, my husband and I decided to try to make our marriage work once again. We were a happy family for some time.

Then suddenly, everything changed. I found out that my husband was going to have to go back to Mexico to get his green card so that he could become a permanent resident. I couldn't handle losing him. He was the only person I had ever felt really loved me. He meant everything to me, and losing him was like losing a part of myself. I wasn't close with my family, so he was really the only family I had. I became very depressed, and one day, while my husband was at work, I decided to kill myself. I wrote a suicide note and called my parents to pick up my son. When they came to pick him up, I gave them the note and told them not to read it until they got home. They suspected that something was wrong and read the note. The police came and took me to the hospital. My suicide attempt had failed. At the hospital, the doctors were able to pump my stomach and get all of the medication I had taken out of my body. I once again had to stay at the hospital until they decided it was safe to send me home. In the suicide note, I had written that I gave custody of my son to my mother. While I was still in the hospital, she took the note to family court and was able to gain custody of my son. I was angry and hurt that she had done that. I wouldn't realize until years later that when I attempted to take my own life, I had in fact abandoned my son. My son was one year old when I lost custody of him.

Finally, it came time for my husband to be sent back to Mexico. I couldn't handle it. I felt like I had lost everything that I loved in this world. The day he left, I was numb, so I just said goodbye and let him go. It would be three years before he was able to come back.

During this time, I became more and more depressed. I began seeing a psychiatrist, and this doctor had prescribed me Xanax to deal with my anxiety. One night, when I was at a friend's house, I was very nervous because I was around people I didn't know, so I started popping the medication. I must have taken about six of them, and I became really high. I enjoyed the feeling of escape that I got when taking the Xanax. Somehow, while under this influence, I injured my neck. I went to the doctors, and they prescribed me Vicodin, a narcotic painkiller. The mixture of the two medications made me really high, and I loved the feeling of being completely numb. When I was under the influence of these two medications, I felt no emotional pain; I just felt really good. It didn't take long before I was going out and drinking as well as taking the medication. I made friends that enjoyed getting drunk and high as well. Soon, getting wasted all the time became my life. I was also very promiscuous and would have one one-night stand after another, but I would always feel horrible when I woke up the next morning. I could not stand to look at myself, which led me to taking even more medication.

My life continued to go downhill. Once again, I tried to kill myself by overdosing on these medications. I was put in the hospital and told that if I wanted to get my son back, I would need to get treatment. So, after about two years of living a drug-addicted existence, I checked myself into a rehab center and worked on getting clean. In the rehab center, I was one of many people who had been using drugs to numb emotional pain. I made some friends there and tried to concentrate on getting to the root of the problem that had made me use drugs to begin with. After twenty-eight days in rehab, I went on to a women's rehab center. It was a little far from where I lived, so I wasn't able to see my son. I really missed being around him. Even when I was doing drugs, I would always stay sober enough so that I could spend time with my son. I couldn't handle not seeing him at all. I called my parents from the rehab center and asked them if I could go home, and they agreed and came to pick me up. While living with them, I was able to spend more time with my son. Finally, things seemed to be going well again.

Chapter Three

❦

After a year of living at my parents house, I still did not have custody of my son. While living at my parent's house, I was able to see him every day and care for him. Things were going really well, and I seemed to be back on track...until I ran into an old friend who asked me if I wanted to move in with her. I agreed, even though I knew she would not be a good influence on me. It wasn't long before I was drinking and doing drugs again. I started going out every weekend and running into even more people I had known. Eventually, things between my roommate and I started to go sour. She moved out, and I took over the apartment. My house became a major party place.

It seemed to be the happening place, and at least once a day, every one of my friends would come over. I felt important because so many people wanted to hang out with me. I was even selling drugs for extra income, yet I was oblivious to the fact that I was helping to ruin the lives of others.

I wanted to do something besides just partying all the time, so I decided to go back to college. During this time, I had visitation with my son, where my mom talked to me about giving custody of my son back to me, and I was really excited and tried to prepare for him to come home. It wasn't long before I was missing days at college and had to drop out because my partying was still so important to me. A friend had introduced me to snorting morphine, and I became addicted right away. I had to call my mom and tell her that I couldn't take my son back because I had ruined my life yet again. That was one of the hardest decisions I have ever had to make, but I knew it wasn't fair to bring him into the mess I had made of my life.

At this point, my parting had become out of control. I was experimenting with different drugs, snorting coke, tripping on acid, and even crack. On New Year's Eve, I went out partying with my friends to celebrate. I had been drinking since early in the day, as well as popping pills, snorting coke, and smoking marijuana. That night, I was raped. I went to the hospital and reported the rape. I was surprised that hardly anyone stood by me when I was going through this. This abandonment gave me even more reason to get wasted. To forget what had happened, I was going out to bars more frequent and doing as many drugs as I could. About a month later, after leaving a bar, I was jumped by four girls and a guy. I got punched in the eye, hit in the head with a beer bottle, and kicked in the face. I went to the hospital and reported the assault to the police. When all of this happened, I had been working at a good job. I was up for a promotion, which gave me the opportunity to move out of town. I decided to leave town to get away from everything; I couldn't handle fighting these two criminal cases and just needed to start over somewhere else.

I moved away and began to start life over. At this point in time, my husband had returned and was staying with my parents. As she had promised, my mom gave me back custody of my son. I continued to smoke marijuana on occasion, and when my son was with his dad, I would go out on the weekends. I went back to school and was working full time, and I was able to keep my partying to a minimum so that I could focus on work and school. My son seemed to be adjusting nicely to being back with me, and we were doing well together. One day, after having a heart to heart with my husband, we decided to give our marriage another chance. I moved back home to the town where most of my abuse had happened. It wasn't long before my husband and I gave up on our marriage once more. At this time, we were both living at my parents' house. Being back in the town where so much had happened to me and feeling the pain from the injustice I had experienced, I decided to start fighting my two assault cases again. The case in which I was jumped was settled by giving each person involved a misdemeanor charge. That made me furious, as I felt that they should have been charged with gang assault. The case of the rape was still pending, and no one had been arrested. I became so depressed that I stayed in bed for two weeks, doing nothing but feeling sorry for myself. Because of this, I ended up losing my job. I also had taken a leave from college. Thankfully, a good friend came by to help bring me out of my depression. At this point in time, I could not see that I was responsible for what had happened to me. I did not want to accept that my drinking and drug use had led to these incidents.

> My body is weak and my mind confused;
> I walk in dark shadows all day long.
> Life barely sustains me,
> Judgments ring in my ears,
> Inadequacies linger in my thoughts.
> I can see happiness in the distance,
> Or is it just a mirage?

While staying at my mom's, my living situation was not working out, so I needed to move. However, I had nowhere to go and no money to get a place, so I became homeless. My son was still staying at my mom's with his dad. On my own, I realized that without a job, I would need to earn some quick money, so I went out of town and stripped to get money. I couldn't do this without being trashed. One night, I made the choice to get into my car while I was intoxicated and try to drive home. On the way home, I ended up in the median and was charged with a DWI. Once again, I had hit the bottom. I realized that something had to change. I couldn't remain on this path of disaster. With the help of an agency, I found a place to live in an isolated area away from all the things that had happened to me. Together, my son and I began to start life over.

Chapter Four

❧

Fortunately, I was able to get a job as a secretary at an agency that I used to work for, but to do so, I needed a babysitter to watch my son for one hour when he got off the bus after school. I called the school, and the school counselor suggested that one girl from a family close to where I lived could possibly watch my son. This is when God intervened in my life, and He worked through this family. Every day after school, this young lady would watch my son until I got home from work. Through talking with her, we began a friendship that would change my life forever.

Once more, my husband and I tried to make our marriage work, but we eventually decided to separate. Shortly after separating, I found out that I was pregnant. We remained friends, but he was sent out of the country for his job.

REDEMPTION

I was drowning in quicksand
When You graciously offered me Your hand,
Sending me on a different course,
One where there would be no remorse.
Now, I'm living life with purpose,
All because You could see beyond the surface
To a soul in need of redeeming,
And so, You filled my life with meaning.
Although there are days still that I feel like giving up
When the pain and raging emotions make me feel as if I've had enough,
It's You and Your Word that keep me grounded,
Even when irrational thoughts have me surrounded.
You're the One solid thing in this life I've been given,

And You're the One that keeps me still driven.

During this season of life, I was let go from my job, so I no longer needed this young lady to watch my son. Our friendship blossomed, and I shared with her that I was pregnant. Her family invited my son and me to go to church with them. I told them that I wasn't ready to go but that I wanted my son to know God. They then started taking my son to church. They continued to ask me to go to church with them, but I said no and told them that I still wasn't ready. I felt that I couldn't be "that good" and that people at church had not lived the type of life I had lived. I didn't feel that I belonged there.

This wonderful family invited me to come to their house to join a group that was learning Spanish. I soon learned how amazing these people were. I had never met people like them before. I felt their love. I couldn't understand how they could accept and love me knowing my past. They explained that the love they had for me came from Christ. During my pregnancy, I decided to go to church and began reading *The Purpose Driven Life.* I soon realized that God loved and accepted me and so would others. I started to feel close to God, and He helped me mend relationships with my family members. I was at peace and happy. I felt amazing, like someone had wiped my past away.

I gave birth to a beautiful little girl, and all of these wonderful friends were there to support me. For a short time, my husband came back from work and then had to leave again. While he was away, I spoke with one of my friends about my marriage. My husband and I still loved each other; we just struggled to make it work. My friend told me that a husband and wife should be together and work out their problems. I felt God calling me to go back to my husband. I talked with my husband about this, and he agreed to give our marriage another chance.

THE REVELATION

Putting an end to inner self-mutilation,
Helping others be free of a relative situation,
Ending relentless emotions that wouldn't cease,
Showing there is hope and peace.
Re-shaping the internal mess,

Learning to live with less stress,

Getting of the emotional roller coaster ride,

Finally entering the other side,

Retaining a sense of calm,

Releasing it into a Psalm,

Bringing healing to a crippling condition,

While creating a beautiful rendition.

Chapter Five

❧

I t was a little over ten years ago that I first began to write this book. When it came time to go forward with the book, trouble hit my home once again. The book would have to be put on pause as I continued to write my poetry throughout the next several years of my struggle. I came face to face with my biggest battle thus far in my life.

It started with no warning. I became ill, and my hair thinned out of my head in a single instant. The next few weeks were filled with varying symptoms of dizziness, weakness, and an overall unwell feeling. This continued for some time with no concrete answer from physicians of what could be causing my symptoms. The doctors ran tests and scans, each coming up empty-handed. My doctors and even loved ones didn't believe my suffering because my symptoms were so drastic and would start and stop with no warning or explanation.

I was working part-time as a driver for a medical company. One day, when I was on break, I stopped by my parents' house for a visit. While visiting with my mother, I passed out on her kitchen floor. After this incident, I was unable to walk for three months. Doctors were stumped because there was no physical reason for me to be unable to walk. Still, I could not stand on my own without falling, let alone walk. My husband suddenly became my twenty-four-hour caretaker. He helped me to the bathroom and to shower. It was humiliating, and I struggled to feel as if I would ever find answers. The next years were riddled with even more radical and unexplainable symptoms. I became catatonic, unable to speak or move my body. My husband and children comforted me and cared for me until hours later, when I could once again move and speak. I had symptoms that mimicked a stroke and a heart attack, as well as unexplainable swelling and pain in my limbs and painful rashes that covered my chest.

I was in and out of the ER and the doctor's office on a regular

basis. At this time, I felt very alone in my suffering, and I struggled to feel as if others took my symptoms seriously or if they believed that I was actually as sick as I was.

SOS

If only you knew
The feelings I have inside that render my soul so blue.
The hurt cuts so deep;
Many nights I go without restful sleep.
The images that I see
Are so very vivid to me;
I wrestle with the thoughts to take my life,
Knowing I would leave my children without a mother and my husband without a wife.
It's not the answer; I know this very well.
This pain, deep in my soul, is where it does dwell.
That's why I am holding onto God with all my might;
I'm weary from the struggle but very much still in this fight!

One night in particular, I was in extreme pain. I was curled up in a fetal position, only able to moan because the pain was so great. During this very moment, I came to grow closer in a relationship with Christ. I was completely alone, and there was no one to cry out to for help but God. When I cried out in my suffering to Him, I saw Jesus on the cross. The look on His face told me that I was not alone in my suffering. He was with me and understood my pain. I was comforted knowing that I was not alone and that He was indeed with me.

After being sent to several specialists, I was diagnosed with somatization disorder, in which anxiety from past trauma turns into physical symptoms. Even after the diagnosis, I found that other doctors at the ER and other places were not familiar with my diagnosis and did not have education on how to handle an individual with this disorder. Many doctors felt that this diagnosis meant that the symptoms were in my head or that I was somehow willingly causing them; therefore, seeking medical help for my symptoms became problematic. I was misdiagnosed several times by paramedics. When I was symptomatic, they would see signs of a stroke, a heart attack, or an overdose and treat me accordingly. I was treated for a heart attack and given medication for it even though I was not having one. Another time, when paramedics found me unresponsive, I was treated with overdose medication although I was actually catatonic.

My family and I decided it was in my best interest to treat the symptoms at home as well as we could, rather than going to the ER for help. There were still situations in which I would need to be seen, but I would mostly deal with the symptoms with only my family and my primary care physician. I was also seeing a mental health professional on a regular basis to try to work through the trauma. We found that talking about the trauma in any way would heighten my symptoms. I even began to have very painful menstrual pain during my periods and uncontrollable vomiting. On several occasions, I ended up being admitted to the hospital for treatment from the continued vomiting

One day, when I was doing the dishes, I heard the voice of God in my left ear. He said one word: "good." I didn't know what exactly was happening, but I knew that God had spoken to me and that He had said the word "good," so it was a good thing. About three months later, repressed memories began to come through. The feelings I would get with the memories were so tormenting that I wanted to die. I once again experienced the memory of when I had been raped around the age of four by my biological father in a prison visiting room. The incident caused my heart to stop on the patio of the prison yard. I had been running from my father when my heart stopped. I had grown up always knowing that my heart had stopped at the prison, and my mother had always said that she was upset that my grandmother never sought medical attention for me after a guard had resuscitated me. The memory of the incident had been suppressed up until this point.

Learning of this caused me so much torment, especially since I had worked hard over the years to have a relationship with my biological father. Facing these memories was even harder when the memories revealed that my aunts and grandmother had covered up the incident and accused my stepfather at the time of molesting me. I sometimes wonder if that was why my stepfather turned into a monster, or if he was always going to be a monster. Unfortunately, I will never know because my stepfather Tom is deceased now. After this, I confronted my biological father over the phone about the incident. He denied doing anything, and that was the last time we have spoken. I have forgiven him for what he has done.

As my life goes on, more memories continue to come out, and I feel as if they are haunting me. I can be doing something, and suddenly, I will see myself being attacked. This horrific feeling occurs within my body that makes me want to scrub off my skin.

Through suppressed memories, it was revealed that when I was six years old, my uncle viciously raped me over a course of days. I remember that I was having an argument with my grandmother about Santa Claus and the Easter Bunny after my grandfather's death. She was angry and told me that they were not real. I yelled back at her that she was a liar. She became so upset with me for calling her a liar that she dragged me to her room. There, she found a dress that was too big for me and called one of my uncles to come pick me up. He took me to the house of another uncle that I had never met before, where my uncle and his girlfriend repeatedly attacked me. I was tied to the bed and raped over and over again. He would call me a dirty little girl while he was assaulting me. The last memory of that incident is of me in the backseat of a truck leaving my uncle's house. When I was brought back to my grandmother's, I remember shaking in the corner, terrified. During this difficult time, God spoke to me again; this time, He said, "Remember My promises. I will redeem you."

THE CONSEQUENCES OF SIN

The sins brought upon me

Leave me screaming, "I'll never be free."

As the past replays in my head,

Audio is on, and I can hear everything they said.

Nothing regarding me was considered or asked;

The fact that I was human and could feel must have been masked.

Their own they treated less than trash;

They had no partaking in the aftermath.

At times, it becomes difficult to believe that I am worth something

When so many treated me as if I was nothing.

Chapter Six

⚜

Thanks be to God, I was able to work with one of the specialists that I had seen. He had decided to go into private practice and worked with individuals with trauma. I had called him on his last day of work, and I would begin working with him shortly after. As the memories continued to come to the surface, I continued to have more physical symptoms. The new doctor sent me to a program at a nearby hospital. The program was geared toward teaching skills to those who have been through trauma. While in the program, I learned ways to deal with the memories without them feeling completely overwhelming, like distraction and turning the mind. This two-week program was very structured, and the staff was very attentive. The last two days of the program, I had to call in because I had become very ill with uncontrollable vomiting and ended up being admitted to the hospital. When I realized that the doctor was not taking my disorder into account for my vomiting, I signed myself out of the hospital against medical advice. I slowly recovered at home. Through all of this, I was so confused with my emotions, which were all over the place. Sensing a loss of hope that this would never end and feeling very alone in what I was experiencing, I had many thoughts about whether or not to take my own life. Feeling that I was a burden to my family and others, I reasoned with myself that my family would be better off if I was not here.

From one day to the next, I continued to struggle with the emotions and feelings but fought to make it through them. I didn't want to give up on my family and friends that were rooting for me. Even now, many days have been dark and lonely, yet I always cry out to God to help me get through them. He will do these little amazing things to help me get through the day, like allowing the sun to suddenly shine through the window at a moment when I have lost hope. I will feel my hope renewed and know that I can carry through to the next moment. At times, it is just like that—surviving from one moment to the next, feeling as if I am just barely hanging on to life. Every time, God will carry me through to the next day.

THIS THORN

This thorn in my side,
So deep and full of shame, whom shall I confide?
The troubles at times are great,
Rendering me to believe this is my inevitable fate,
Unending suffering and struggle until the day I die.
To whom shall I rely?
He's been faithfully by my side;
His arms stretch far and wide.
To whom I shall rely
Until the day I die!

MARIONETTE

Screaming for answers and hearing silence in return,
Waiting impatiently for when it's my turn,
Wondering when this hell will end and life will resume,
Feeling as if I am in a play, waiting on my impending doom,
I'm the flimsy puppet hanging from somewhere above,
Waiting on the One with the power to cut the strings and
return me to His love,
Wanting to take back control and instead receiving
no resolve,
Realizing maybe it was never my problem to try and solve.
How foolish of me to think that I could win
When I continue to fight the wrong battle, the one within.

After recovering from my hospital stay, I missed being
in the group atmosphere, where I really felt like I was with
people who were like me. I bonded with them on a very
real level. We had a very strict rule on not exchanging
information with each other, so because I ended up in the
hospital at the end, I was never able to say goodbye. I still

think about the people I met there and pray that they are doing well.

Going back to therapy has had its challenges. I constantly feel as if I am backsliding—two steps forward, four steps back. The physical symptoms are beginning to improve, but the memories will come all at once, flooding me with more information than I can handle knowing. I crumble under the weight of the memories. The memories have a way of taking me back to the situation as if it is happening to me in the present. I feel scared and have a magnitude of feelings that are too much to bear at times. My strongest desire is for someone to take these things away and have them not be real. However, I have learned that denying the existence of the memories causes them to become stronger. As much as I don't want to face that reality, I have to. If I want to move on with my life, then I need to accept the existence and truth of the experiences that these memories represent. I can't change the things that happened to me. I can, however, change the way I react to these memories, with hard work and dedication. The road has been long, but God has been with me every step of the way.

JEHOVAH EL EMETH (LORD GOD OF TRUTH)

I give You willingly my heart;

It was only You who knew me from the very start.

You always knew my inner thoughts and things I desire,

Watching over me with an endearing love I can only admire.

Thank you, Father, for never abandoning me,

Especially in the times I clearly could not see.

When I took the wrong road

After I was clearly told

Because I refused to see,

Still, You continue to love me.

Even now, You're freeing me from a painful past,

And when the joyful moments don't always last,

I know, without a doubt, in the end, I'll be free

Because it's a promise You made to me.

CPSIA information can be obtained
at www.ICGtesting.com
Printed in the USA
LVHW081211300720
661938LV00002B/401

9 781631 297427